MAGNIFICENT MEHNDI DESIGNS

COLORING BOOK

COLOR
DOODLE
IMAGINE
CREATE

LINDSEY BOYLAN
MARTY NOBLE

DOVER PUBLICATIONS, INC.
MINEOLA, NEW YORK

Beautiful paisleys make up this detailed coloring collection showcasing designs reminiscent of the ancient practice of mehndi body art. A unique opportunity for the experienced colorist, over 125 illustrations provide limitless possibilities for experimentation. Plus, perforated pages make displaying your work easy.

Bibliographical Note

Magnificent Mehndi Designs Coloring Book, first published by Dover Publications, Inc., in 2015, is a republication in one volume of the following previously published Dover books: *Mehndi Designs Coloring Book* (2013), *Magnificent Mehndi Designs Coloring Book* (2015), and *Magical Mehndi Coloring Book* (2015). Artwork for plates 1–64 by Marty Noble; artwork for plates 65–127 by Lindsey Boylan.

International Standard Book Number

ISBN-13: 978-0-486-80873-4
ISBN-10: 0-486-80873-4

Manufactured in the United States by RR Donnelley
80873401   2015
www.doverpublications.com

Exsprpss

Exsprpss

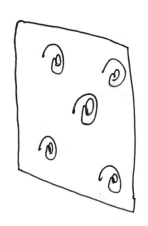